KIDSBIZ

Tracy Marsh

TRACY MARSH PUBLICATIONS

"Some of the most successful businesses began as hobbies!"

Contents

The bottom line

Let's face it. You need money for clothes, for music, for going out, for doing the kinds of things you enjoy doing.

Your parents are tired of you bugging them for money.

But right now you're at an age where you're stuck between running a neighborhood lemonade stand and getting your first real job.

What do you do?

Go into business for yourself by starting your own!

It's not as tricky as it sounds, and it can be a great experience that will benefit you in the future.

Not only could you make money, you'll gain real work experience, make contacts, and be able to use your business skills as a valuable addition to future job applications by listing them on your résumé.

Tips of the trade

The first step to success is choosing a business that's right for you! There's an old saying "Do what you love and the money will follow", so it's important that the business you set up is based on an activity you enjoy doing – and it helps if it's something you're good at too!

As you read through this book, study the Business Plan for each business idea proposed. You'll get a gut feeling for whether the business is something that would suit you and your individual talents. The Business Plan will also help you work out practicalities such as how to go about marketing your business, whether you can afford the set-up costs, who your potential customer base is, and what risks might be involved!

You must be able to make a profit from your business. You will need to be able to manage a budget as well as set the correct prices – and stick to them!

Adjust your attitude. If you go in thinking you're going to be successful, then potential customers will be caught up in your drive and enthusiasm. Be prepared to work hard and show dedication, and you will reap the rewards!

There are lots of other factors to consider when launching a new business. They differ for each business idea and are outlined in the pages to come. You'll find that there are all sorts of exciting challenges and creative ideas just waiting for you to tap into them.

You need to find customers! Spread the word through family and friends that you're open for business. Get promoting, because without customers you won't have a business!

Tools of the trade

One of the keys to success is having the right equipment.

It's important to think ahead in terms of set-up and ongoing costs. For example, you don't want to find out you've lost money because you ran up a huge cell phone bill. Here is some equipment you might need:

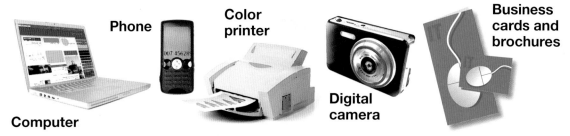

Computer   **Phone**   **Color printer**   **Digital camera**   **Business cards and brochures**

Business name. Think of a unique name that represents your business. You want it to be memorable so that it jumps out at people. Be clever but remain professional.

Business cards and a brochure that outlines your product or services. First impressions are important. Great design and copy can convey to potential customers that you take your business seriously and have invested time and money in promotion.

Rules of the trade

Make sure a parent or other adult family member knows exactly what you intend to do with your business. You might like to nominate that person as your business consultant. Keep him or her informed of your progress and if anything happens that makes you uncomfortable, or if you feel you need help with something, make sure to tell your business consultant immediately.

You could also have a parent or responsible adult act as an employee and accompany you on any necessary field trips for your business. He or she can come in very handy adjusting lights, carrying equipment, and handing out flyers.

Most importantly, always make sure a parent or other adult knows where you are and how you can be contacted.

Talk of the trade

The business world uses its own lingo, which you will need to understand and use. Here is a list of some of the terms you may come across along with their definitions.

Bookkeeping
The process of recording the amounts of money coming into the business and going out.

Budget
A plan that gives an estimate of the expenses and profit required to make the business a success.

Cash flow
The amount of money coming into and going out of the business.

Copyright
A law that protects words and ideas such as those in books, movies, photographs, creative ideas, drawings, and music from being used by anyone without permission from the copyright owner.

Discount
A deduction made from the cost or purchase price.

Entrepreneur
A person who finds opportunities in everything he or she does – like turning a hobby into a business!

Expenses
The costs incurred by the business so that it can operate effectively.

Financing
Money obtained to start or expand the business.

Financier or Investor
The person or bank who gives the initial money to start or expand the business. In this case it could be your parents!

Income
The money that comes into the business from sales.

Investment
Money used to purchase items for the business to help make a profit, such as new software or a better camera.

Invoice
A written document made out to a customer showing the cost of goods or work completed.

Marketing
The advertising and promotion of a product or service.

Markup
The difference between the price of the original materials (cost price) and the price you sell the finished item at (retail price), often expressed as a percentage.

Net profit
The amount of money you have left from a sale after expenses have been deducted.

Partnership
A business relationship between two or more people who share the business responsibilities, profits, and risk. Could be your best friend or sister!

Stock
The items you have made that are for sale.

Wholesale
The cost of items when you are selling them to stores for those stores to resell.

Selling secondhand

Do you and your friends have stuff lying around that you no longer use? What if you could sell your old toys, games, books, CDs and DVDs as a starting point for a business venture? Remember – one person's trash is another person's treasure!

Business Plan

Overview
Sell or trade secondhand books, games, CDs, DVDs and just about anything you can think of! You can sell your own stuff and also make money by selling for other people.

The Customer
Friends, family, or anyone who wants to purchase, sell, or trade items they no longer have a need for.

Cost to set up
You might need to purchase some stock in order to get started.

Risk
You could get left with product that doesn't sell. You need to make sure you purchase or trade popular items that will sell quickly.

Tools of the trade
You'll need access to a computer if you want to create a catalog, set up a web site, or edit photos.

Rule
Make sure a parent or other adult knows exactly what you are doing at all times.

Start with the items you no longer use and build from there!

Toys

Comic books

Music equipment like MP3 players

Electronic games

Sports equipment

CDs and DVDs

Books

Trading cards

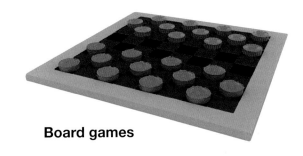

Board games

 # Talking cents

Before setting up your business you need to come up with a price structure for each transaction. Research what the item is worth, when purchased new. Decide on a fair and reasonable selling price taking into account wear and age. You may find that one fifth of the original price is a good starting point.

If you've bought an item intending to resell it, then you need to price this item in order for you to make a profit. Try adding 50% to the price you paid. For instance, if you bought it for $10, you could resell for $15.

If you're selling for other people, then you need to set a fee for your service or take a percentage of the sale for each item sold.

purchase items at 1/5 original price add 50% to resell $3 trading fee or % of sale

Marketing your business

Set up your own web site or catalog and list all the items you have for sale alongside their price. Look at Amazon and eBay for ideas and inspiration. Remember it's not just the item that's important but the way you sell it – so use your imagination!

Photograph and write out a description for each item you are selling.

To promote your business, print out business cards and brochures listing all the items you have for sale and e-mail or hand them out to prospective customers.

Business ideas

You might want to think about specializing. If you're an avid reader, you could specialize in selling books. The same goes for music, toys, DVDs. If you sound like you know the product, then people will be more likely to buy from you. It also means you're less likely to be left with stock that won't sell as you will have a better idea of the market.

Think about selling hard-to-find or rare items such as trading cards or stamps.

Tips of the trade

Be sure to thoroughly test your products before offering them for sale. If you're selling CDs and DVDs make sure they're in good working order. The last thing you want is an unsatisfied customer who wants his or her money back.

Before you know it you will be buying, selling, and trading successfully!

Hot off the press

If you're a whiz on the computer, then why not try your hand at designing newsletters for your local sports teams or community organizations.

Business Plan

Overview

Produce regular newsletters for groups such as sports teams, clubs, local businesses, or familes planning special events.

The Customer

Any organization that has a need to regularly promote its activities.

Cost to set up

You will need paper, inks, envelopes, postage, and possibly some computer software.

Risk
Minimal risk other than the initial set-up cost.

Tools of the trade
Access to a computer and printer. If you are helping with the content of the newsletter, you may need a scanner and camera.

Rule
Make sure a parent or other adult knows where you are at all times.

Business ideas

You could offer a service that will produce, print out, and mail a newsletter. Alternatively you could set up an electronic mailing list and offer a service that will send the newsletter out by e-mail.

Many organizations produce a newsletter on a regular basis. Often the responsibility for writing and printing the newsletter falls to someone who doesn't have the necessary time and throws it together at the last moment. This is where you can step in.

Consider gathering sponsorship to cover your costs by placing a company's advertisement in your publication. You will need to get permission first from the group you are printing the newsletter for.

Marketing your business

A good way to set up the business and to gather a client base is to work for free initially in exchange for advertising your services in the newsletter you are distributing.

Talking cents

Make sure you correctly estimate the costs you will incur. Ink cartridges for printers – especially color ink cartidges – are expensive. Call several local photocopying services and compare prices for bulk copies.

Your aim is to have regular work as opposed to doing one-shot jobs. Consider offering a discount on your services after a certain number of jobs done. This type of discount is perhaps best known as the "coffee card" – after ten cups you get one free. It is a proven formula for success.

Tips of the trade

If the organization you are working for does not have a dedicated person whose role it is to gather the information for the newsletter, you can slowly make yourself indispensable by taking on more and more responsibility.

Masthead

Issue number

Advertisements

Subheads

Headline

Feature article

Start out by printing and delivering and as you get to know the group's business, make suggestions and offer solutions. You might even want to offer to take photographs that could be included. Does the newsletter have a catchy name and a logo? If not, come up with one!

Add interesting elements to the newsletter such as puzzles, crosswords, contests, little-known facts and statistics, even a funny cartoon!

Teaching technology

There are lots of adults, particularly elderly people, who have few basic technology skills. Working a television remote or programming a new cell phone can seem very daunting to them. This is where you step in! A great business opportunity is sharing your knowledge and teaching technology.

Business Plan

Overview

Teach others some basic to high-tech skills such as surfing the Net, e-mail, tips for cell phones, even the use of certain computer programs like Word or Excel.

The Customer

Anyone who has trouble learning to use technology.

Cost to set up

No real cost involved in setup. You may find printouts useful for step-by-step tutorial purposes.

Risk

No risk other than you testing your frustration levels. Be patient!

Tools of the trade

Access to a computer and the necessary technical equipment and software so that you are proficient in what you are teaching.

Rule

Make sure a parent or other adult knows exactly what you are doing at all times.

Business ideas

There's a huge technological world out there!
A few ideas to get you started:

Computer skills

Imagine what it must be like to use a computer for the
first time. You could start with turning the computer on
and off, logging on,editing, saving, moving files, how to
use various programs, how to browse the Internet,
how to save favorite sites, and e-mail.

Cell phones

Texting, shortcuts, predictive text, contacts, ring tones,
settings, taking photos, forwarding, address book,
business cards, downloading to a computer, access
to Internet, and using cell phones overseas.

TV/DVD

Using a remote control,
adjusting volume, changing
stations, tuning stations,
plugging in and using a DVD
player to play and to record.

Other equipment

Printer, fax machine, scanner, digital
camera and video camera, even a CD
player as opposed to a record player!

Marketing your business

Word of mouth could be powerful for this kind of business. As your client base isn't necessarily online, you might need to print out flyers and drop them in mailboxes in your neighborhood. Remember to run everything you do past a parent or other adult!

Heads up

"Make sure you have done the necessary research and can express yourself well. It's one thing to be able to use technology, but another thing entirely to teach it."

Talking cents

It would be ideal if you could find regular customers who would come back to you again and again. Think about how you can make yourself indispensable from the start. You can advertise as someone who is there to help in the research, purchase, initial setup, use, and maintenance of new technical equipment.

You may even want to set an exam for the end of each tutorial.

Another way of helping someone to learn is by giving that person real scenarios to take away and practice. Yes! You can give homework. It's payback time!

Either charge a flat fee for the lesson or charge by the hour.

21

Be a hotshot

If you have a talent for taking great photos, then why not turn your hobby into a business! You could take portraits of families or pets, submit photos to newspapers, magazines, or photography contests, display your favorite shots at an exhibit, make greeting cards, or record special occasions such as weddings, parties, school plays, or sports events.

Business Plan

Overview
Take photographs at weddings, parties, family gatherings, school plays, sports events, or even tourist attractions. You could focus on portraits of families or their pets.

The Customer
Will depend on the type of photographer you choose to be. You could do assignment photography and take photos for people or sell your own photos on a freelance basis.

Cost to set up
Need access to a digital camera, computer, and printer. There will also be a cost for the photographic paper and inks.

Risk
Not much financial risk, but you could get bitten if you choose pet photography!

Tools of the trade
Start with a basic digital camera. As your business grows, you can invest in a better camera and more equipment such as lights and a tripod.

Rule
Get a parent or other adult to accompany you, if you are going on location.

Business ideas

Your first step is to determine whether you will specialize in one particular type of photography or diversify with assignment or freelance photography.

Assignment photography means taking portraits or candid shots at weddings, parties, and school functions. Freelance photography means taking photos and selling them to newspapers and magazines, local businesses, tourist organizations, schools, and even friends and family.

Tourist photographs

Take photos of a famous landmark in your area that might be of use to tourist agencies or web sites. If you go away on vacation, take photos of what interests you, and you may find that those photos are also interesting to a magazine or other publication.

Portrait photography

Parents love to have photos of their kids at any and every age. Think about ways you can make your portraits more interesting than what is currently available. What is a unique way you can represent the person being photographed?

Pet photography

Every pet owner needs someone else to take a perfect photograph of him or her with that special loved one. You can charge for your time as well as offering the printed photo and digital image.

School events

Offer to capture significant moments at school events such as atheletic contests, graduations, and plays. You could sell your services to individuals or to the school.

Local community events

Take your camera with you to festivals, community days, and parades. You could sell prints to family members performing or taking part in a parade or to local newspapers.

Current affairs

Take photographs of exciting or history-making events in your area and sell them to newspapers, magazines, or local government organizations.

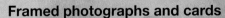

Special occasions

Offer your photographic skills at weddings, parties, and family events.

Framed photographs and cards

If you think you have a group of exceptional photographs that work together nicely as a series, you could frame them to sell or use them to create a selection of greeting cards.

Marketing your business

One of the best ways to show your style and versatility is to have a portfolio. It's like a résumé but in photographs. It shows prospective clients what they can expect from the kind of work you do.

Your portfolio can be printed out in an album or you could create a digital slideshow presentation on CD or DVD for your potential customers!

You can use your own photo printing software at home or use a photo processing service.

Talking cents

Be careful not to set too high a price for your photos when you first start out. If you really enjoy taking pictures, then treat your early assignments as a training ground. You do want to make sure you cover the costs of your materials and get some form of re-imbursement for your time, however.

Cover the cost of materials and your time.

Heads up
"Make sure you get permission to film locations, events, and people before photographing them".

Tips of the trade

 Don't be afraid to experiment. Some of the most unusual effects have been discovered by accident! The great thing about digital photos is that you can always delete them.

If you're not sure where to begin with your photography then start at home with people you know. You can experiment by taking candid and posed shots of your family and friends – and don't be shy about asking them for their feedback.

Turn off your digital zoom. It only gets you grainy photos. Digital zoom just means blowing up the photo. It doesn't bring you closer to the action or capture more detail. You're better off using optical zoom on a high-quality picture setting and cropping the photo on the computer at a later date.

Shutter lag is the time it takes for most digital cameras to focus and calculate the exposure after you have pressed the shutter button but before the shot is captured. You can usually eliminate the shutter lag by half-pressing the shutter button before the action begins. The camera pre-focuses and locks in those settings, as long as you continue to half-press the shutter button.

Playing with light can have dramatic results in your photography.

Here are some useful tips about lighting:

* If you are taking photos in direct midday sunshine, move your subject into the shade or indoors near a window. Direct sunlight creates unflattering deep shadows.

* Side window lighting is always flattering. Position your subject next to a window and watch how the soft light helps produce an attractive image.

* The best time to take outdoor photos is when it's overcast.

Magnetic attraction!

shut the door

Help save our planet... It's the only one with chocolate

Happy Holidays
The Keane Family

When you think of magnets, you probably think of local businesses whose logos and details are holding up bills and photos on your refrigerator. Promoting a business is just one use for magnets! They can be used as invitations or thank you's, and even for inspirational messages.

Business Plan

Overview
Handmade magnets for personal use and to promote businesses.

The Customer
Local businesses, sports teams, clubs, family, and friends.

Cost to set up
You will need to purchase a few craft supplies in order to make the magnets.

Risk
Minimal, other than the initial cost to make up samples of your product.

Tools of the trade
Computer and printer.

Rule
Make sure a parent or other adult knows exactly what you are doing at all times.

How to make magnets

You will need

- Small wood or thick card-stock shapes
- Acrylic paint and brush
- Scissors
- Decoupage glue
- Instant decoupage resin or sealer
- Precut adhesive magnetic squares

1 Paint the wood or card-stock shapes on one side and around the edges and leave them to dry.

2 Create your magnet design on the computer, slightly smaller in size than the wood or card-stock shapes. Duplicate the design on one sheet to save on paper, and print out.

3 Cut out the design. Glue them onto the unpainted side of the wood or card-stock shapes.

4 Coat the designs with instant decoupage resin or sealer and leave them to set properly.

5 Attach a precut adhesive magnetic square to the back of each magnet shape.

Marketing your business

In addition to selling your magnets to local businesses, friends, and family, you could also sell them at craft fairs and flea markets or to sports teams and clubs as a fundraiser – they can resell them to raise money for their organizations.

Talking cents

Depending on the size and quality of your magnets, you might charge anywhere between $2 and $4 per magnet.

Give a discount for bulk orders!

Heads up

"You must get permission before using any logos or business names."

Business ideas

Invitations
Birthdays, weddings, or any special event can be displayed on magnets. Those who receive them will never forget the date!

Spread the word
Make others aware of world issues, environmental challenges, or local concerns with handmade magnets that people will buy from you. The great thing about this business idea is that while you are making a few dollars, you are also making a difference!

Baby announcements
A magnet makes a really nice keepsake for the announcement of a new baby's arrival.

Sports teams and clubs
Your local organizations might buy magnets to promote their team or club. Make them to order or make up a few and sell them.

Advertising for local businesses
Approach your local businesses and community organizations and offer to make magnets to promote their product or service.

Christmas cards
Magnets make novel greeting cards that can be displayed on a refrigerator or filing cabinet.

Special occasions
Refrigerator magnets make a great thank you and serve as a memento of weddings, parties, or any special occasion.

Author extraordinaire

Have you always wanted to write a book?
Stop daydreaming and start writing! You could take on
the role of publisher, writing and publishing your own work.
Whether it's a children's book or for adults, fiction or
nonfiction, long or short, it will have a market.
So don't wait any longer, get your ideas down on paper!

Business Plan

Overview
Write and self-publish books.

The Customer
Anyone who enjoys reading great books!

Cost to set up
Writing is inexpensive but it does take up
a lot of time. The printing of the books
could be expensive if you are not able to
do it at home and need to pay for digital
printing and binding.

Risk
You can invest lots of time in
researching and writing without any
guarantee of success, but if you don't
try you will never know!

Tools of the trade
Most tasks involved in self-publishing
– the research, writing, illustrations and
photographs – can be achieved using
a computer.

Business ideas

Choosing what to write about can seem overwhelming at first. Where should you begin?

Start by choosing a subject you are passionate about and one that you have knowledge of. It could be your favorite sport, jokes, or funny stories. Think about what you and your friends are interested in, or like to read, and go from there.

Short stories

Writing a novel might seem like a huge project, so why not try writing short stories? Try out different genres to see which one suits your writing style best. Some examples are romance, horror, science fiction, mystery/detective, historical fiction – or wherever your imagination happens to take you!

Children's storybook

If you can write, illustrate, and tell a good story that appeals to the imagination of a young children, then you can write children's books. If you wanted to personalize a story for an individual, you could include the name of the child in the story.

You can also play with writing techniques such as point of view. Are you going to tell the story from the narrator's perspective or from the perspective of the main character? Will it be told in real time or in the future looking back? You have lots to think about!

Heads up

"It's easier to self-publish your work than it is to get it published through a publisher!"

Autobiography

Although most autobiographies are written by famous people, there is no need to let that stop you from writing yours! It might be as simple as keeping a journal and writing about your hopes and dreams. Perhaps something remarkable happened to you that others will find inspirational or fascinating. Hey – you might not sell many, but you'll certainly learn a lot about yourself in the process.

Noodle soup

1 ll dip et irlit irll iriustrud
2 exeros alit at iusciila alit
1 vel do erci bla
feugue minci er irliqu
ipsustis nos niam
7 am in heniamcon velssectet.
quat wisse do
dipiscilit nis alit adio

dunt delit aut augue magna adipsustin
essequam duisl ulla feu facing endre mod
doloreet ing at wissequat, volum zzrit vel
ullam, quate magnis nisim zzriure commy
nonsequi ex exero od eum dolorem essi.
Cum ipit ipsusto consequi tat.
Mod min henis nisi ullaor sequiss
equametummy nisiscidunt laor si.
Vulput acipsum in henissenim eros ad
moluptate tio od te tatetum ea commy non
velestrud ea facil iu

Cookbook

Gather together your favorite recipes as well as those of your friends or your family!
Prepare each of the recipes, photograph them, and make them up into a book.
Many famous chefs started out with a love of cooking and documented their dishes.

Joke book

If you have a talent for telling a funny story or a good joke,
then gather those stories and jokes together and publish a
book of them so that everyone can share the laughs!
You could even add some funny pictures or photos.

Your family history

Researching and writing your own family history is a great idea! If you have a large family, then there will be plenty of people to buy the books! There are web sites that can guide you through the process of compiling your family ancestry.

It could be lots of fun interviewing different family members and uncovering aspects of your family you knew nothing about. You may even find some dark hidden secret!

How-to book

How about writing a book about your favorite craft or hobby? It could be anything from scrapbooking to gardening to building model airplanes. You will need to think about the layout of your book. It should include step-by-step instructions along with illustrations and photographs of your subject.

Marketing your business

Depending on the subject, you can try selling your books to friends, family, or even your local bookstore. You could submit your book to the local newspaper; if they write a favorable review, then you could soon have publishers knocking on your door!

Make sure you don't sell your books for less than they are worth!

Talking cents

If it's possible to print and bind your books at home, then this is the cheapest option. If not, investigate your local digital printer or office suppliers who can print small print runs at a reasonable cost.

Pricing your books will depend on their size and number of pages, and what they cost to produce.

Heads up

"Ask someone to read a draft of your book before you go to print. It helps to have an outside eye assess your work. He or she might pick up things you hadn't even thought of!"

Tips of the trade

✔ Try to find out which publishers accept manuscripts and send a copy of your book to them. Many now famous authors were discovered from the "slush pile".

✔ Learn about your genre by reading those who write it best. If mysteries are your passion, make sure you've read some examples of good and bad detective stories. You'll learn from both.

✔ Find out when the next writer's festival is coming to your city. You'll be inspired by hearing some of your favorite authors sharing the story of their struggles. You might even make some valuable contacts.

✔ Try to sign up for a writing class or join a writers' workshop. These can be valuable when you're just starting out. You'll also meet others who have the same goals as you.

✔ Start or join a book club. You'll gain friends who also love books and learn more about the process of critiquing writing and what it takes to construct a well-written story.

✔ Try to get an unpaid internship at a publisher whose work you admire. You'll be amazed at how much you learn about an industry from spending some time on the inside.

When in doubt, keep writing! It can be lonely at times, but your perseverance and passion will pay off!

✔ Seeing your book in print can be really satisfying and will usually make all the hard work worthwhile. Whatever the subject, if you really feel you have something meaningful to write about, this could be a very successful business and the beginning of a wonderful career.

friends forever

Printworks

Have you ever seen a really cool design on a shirt and wished you had one just like it? It might say something really out there, or it might be a message about making a difference in the world. You could set up a business making your own slogans and designs on the computer, print multiple shirts and sell them!

Business Plan

Overview
Print customized T-shirts or other fabric items for sports teams or local clubs. Print T-shirts with trendy slogans and designs that are unique.

The Customer
Anyone who appreciates unique designs that are fashionable. Sports teams and local clubs or groups.

Cost to set up
You will need to purchase the T-shirts, special paper for printing, and printer inks.

Risk
There is very little risk because you can "print on demand"!

Tools of the trade
A computer, good-quality printer, and inks are essential. You will also need the necessary supplies for printing on fabric.

recycle

friends
forever

Business ideas

Spread the word
Make a difference in the world or in your community with an appropriate message. Cloth bags printed with environmental messages can be sold to stores that will offer the bags for sale rather than using plastic bags.

Cash in
A great way to make money is to cash in on a local event or newsworthy happening.

Go team!
Promote the items you can print on to local sports teams and clubs. You could even print small flags and banners for team supporters.

Cool events
Research events that are coming up around where you live. There might be a particular festival, play, or music concert. Contact the management and pitch yourself as someone who could take care of designing their merchandise.

Photo fun
Photos of people and places can also be printed on fabric. Fun ideas include bride and groom pre-wedding parties, pets on T-shirts or pillows, birthday celebrations, or a "best friends club".

Art on everything!
Don't restrict yourself to printing only on T-shirts. Branch out into designs for bags, aprons, pillowcases, dish towels, caps, or even pillow covers!

Marketing your business

If your aim is to stand out from the crowd, then emphasize the difference between your products and the mass-produced shirts with slogans that "everyone" wears. You want to appeal to the kind of person who appreciates individuality.

You might consider giving some of your favorite designs to people who agree to wear them. Someone looking good in your designs is the best publicity you could ask for!

Talking cents

Make sure you charge enough to cover the cost of the materials and your time, and that there is enough left over for you to make a profit!

A simple formula would be:

cost of materials + 50% = selling price

You could offer clubs and teams a discount for bigger quantities!

**cost of materials
+ 50%
= selling price**

Heads up

"Some T shirt suppliers charge less if you buy in bulk!"

Tips of the trade

If you are marketing yourself to clubs or sports teams make sure the shirts are made of good-quality fabric. One hundred percent cotton would be best if people are going to be breaking a sweat while wearing them!

If possible always get the club or team artwork supplied as a jpeg to make it easier for you to work with and to make sure you are using their exact colors of the logo.

How to print on fabric

What you need

- plain fabric items
- iron-on transfer paper from office suppliers and craft shops
- iron

1 Use a supplied jpeg, photos, type or scans to design your message on the computer.

2 The iron-on transfer paper you will use is fairly expensive, so try to fit at least two or more of the same design on the one piece of paper.

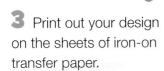

3 Print out your design on the sheets of iron-on transfer paper.

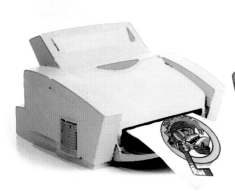

4 Follow the manufacturer's instructions on the package to iron the transfers onto the fabric.

Camera! action!

Rule
Get a parent or other adult to accompany you, if you are going on location.

PROD. NO.
SCENE
TAKE
ROLL
SOU

If you love movies and think you might want to be a filmmaker, then why not offer your services behind the camera? Not only will you gain experience, but you might even make some money at the same time!
So what are you waiting for – lights! camera! action!

Business Plan

Overview
Film and produce DVDs of community events, performances, and special occasions such as birthday parties or weddings.

The Customer
Any person or organization who would like a record of an event or special occasion.

Cost to set up
You need access to a DVD camera, computer, and printer. Cost involved in purchasing writable DVDs and cases.

Risk
Minimal!

Tools of the trade
DVD camera, computer, and printer.

💡 Business ideas

Going local
You could film street parades, parties, community events, ballet performances, or local plays.

School is cool
Offer to capture significant occasions at schools such as athletic events, graduations, debates and plays.

Make every occasion special
Offer your photographic skills at weddings, parties, and family events.

Tools of the trade

The equipment you need will depend on your budget and the type of filming you want to do.

Start with a basic video camera, and as your business grows you could invest some of your profits in a better camera and more equipment such as a tripod, lights and a microphone.

You will also need film-editing software for post production so that you can download the filmed material onto the computer, edit it for the final production, and burn it to DVD. Most digital cameras come with software.

Marketing your business

Having an example of a really dynamic DVD you have already produced is one of the best ways you can market yourself. Carry a few copies around with you so you can hand one to anybody who is interested in your service. You never know when and where you're going to meet a potential client!

Heads up

"Make sure you get permission to film locations, events, and people beforehand."

Talking cents

If you really enjoy the process of making movies then consider your first few assignments an opportunity to gain experience. You'll be surprised at how quickly your work improves with practice. Looking back, you might be glad you didn't charge for the first few jobs.

Always make sure you cover the cost of your materials. Filming events is a very cost-effective business because once you have filmed and edited the DVD, you can burn and sell as many copies as you like.

This is referred to as "making a good profit margin"!

Tips of the trade

✓ Have a thorough knowledge of your equipment and take good care of it. Keep it clean and store it properly.

✓ Hold your camera steady. Nobody likes getting motion sickness from watching a movie! Investing in a tripod can make a difference if you are filming long, still events such as speeches.

✓ Charge your batteries before shooting and always carry spare batteries. You can be guaranteed your battery will go dead at the crucial moment!

✓ Film with the light source behind you. Shooting in a poor light will make your pictures look grainy, out of focus, and colorless.

✓ Practice the use of zooming and panning. Use them both sparingly. Make sure you hold a shot for at least a few seconds before moving on.

✓ Experiment with capturing your subject from different angles. Don't stay wide or close for longer than 15 seconds.

✓ Take a digital camera along on your assignments so that you can take some photographs for the DVD case sleeve. Design a sleeve with a photo or two and a title, and don't forget your name, details, and contact numbers for future business!

✓ Ensure that the date/time stamp remains off. It cannot be removed later but can be added in post production.

Post-production editing

The more features it has, the more professional your film will look and the more attractive it will be to your audience. Include as many of these features as possible in your post-production editing.

Use a title at the beginning.

A set of "shots" cut together is a nice way to tell a story. For example, if you are telling the story of a birthday party, different shots from the event might include:

- the cake
- people at the party
- blowing out the candles

Try interesting transitions between the shots, like fading one shot into another.

Use an appropriate soundtrack and narration.

Use titles to identify people, places, and objects.

Experiment with fast and slow motion as well as real time.

Play your cards right

If you are creative and enjoy working with paper and creating designs on a computer, then this is the business for you! Make unique cards, invitations, and letterheads for local businesses, friends, family, gift shops, and stationery outlets.

Business Plan

Overview
Create personalized stationery, invitations, and greeting cards.

The Customer
Friends, relatives, and local businesses.

Cost to set up
You will need a good-quality printer and card/paper supplies and embellishments.

Risk
Risk involved in being left with unsold stock.

Tools of the trade
Computer and printer.

Business ideas

Create custom-made invitations for weddings, birthday parties, and anniversaries.

Make blank cards for gift and stationery stores to sell.

Create personalized letterhead, business cards, and stationery for individuals and local businesses.

Create a line of wrapping paper to complement your gift cards.

Marketing your business

Make up a brochure or samples displaying your designs and distribute through local gift shops, stationery outlets, bridal stores, friends, and family.

Use your stationery as much as possible in your own life. If your products are good, people will soon be asking for them!

Double your cost price for your selling price

Tips of the trade

Do some research to find out what similar items are selling for in stores and online.

Presentation matters! A nice touch for invitations or stationery is to present them in cellophane bags, in gift boxes, or tied up with ribbon.

Plan ahead and purchase the cards, decorative and colored papers, envelopes, and embellishments as cheaply as possible. Try discount stores, online, and direct from the manufacturers.

Always get a 50% deposit (half the total order) before you lay out the time and money to buy the paper or cards to make the invitations or stationery.

Talking cents

The price at which you would sell to your own customer is the retail price.
A store would charge that same price, so when you sell your designs to a store, charge at half the price at which you would sell to your own customer.

Rule of thumb:
Your cost = $1.00. That cost doubled ($2.00) would be the wholesale cost you would charge the store. The store would sell at twice the wholesale cost, or $4.00 retail. If selling directly to customers, charge the $4.00 retail price.

Heads up

"Don't copy other designs, rely on your own creativity for a successful biz!"

Date with destiny

Everyone needs to know what the current day and date are! Use your creative computer skills and artistic talent to make fun and decorative desk calendars. Whether you market them to businesses or for personal use, you'll find your designs could really take off!

Business Plan

Overview
Create decorative or personalized desk calendars to sell.

The Customer
Friends, relatives, local businesses, or community organizations.

Cost to set up
You will need to purchase some supplies to get started.

Risk
Sales will be seasonal as most people buy calendars toward the end of the year for the next year.

Tools of the trade
Computer and printer.

How to make a desk calendar

What you need:

- 6 squares of thick card stock 71/2" x 71/2' (19cm x 19cm)
- Single-hole punch
- 5 curtain or binder rings
- Paints and a small paintbrush
- Assorted colored papers
- Ribbons
- Embellishments
- Double-sided tape or glue
- Scissors
- Pencil and ruler

Heads up

"You can use thin craft wood instead of thick card stock if you have an adult to help cut the wood and drill the holes."

1 Punch five holes along one edge of each square of card. The holes must be exactly the same distance apart on each piece.

2 Paint around the edges of the 6 pieces and leave them to dry. You can paint them all the same color or different colors.

3 Measure and cut a piece of colored paper for each side of each card stock piece. Use double-sided tape or glue to attach the paper to the card stock. Place the tape or glue around the edges and in the middle.

4 Now you will need the computer and printer to design and print out the calendar months.

5 Lay out a table measuring 4" x 3" (10cm x 8cm) with 7 boxes across the top and 7 boxes down the side.

6 Include a letter for each day of the week starting with 'S' for Sunday.

7 Refer to an existing calendar for the year you are creating and make up a table for each month, inserting the appropriate date in each square.

8 Print out each month.

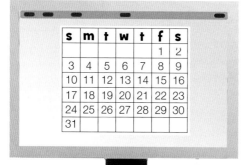

9 Experiment with different font ideas for the months.

JANUARY FEBRUARY march APRIL
MAY JUNE JULY AUGUST
SEPTEMBER NOVEMBER
october DECEMBER

10 Think of different ways you can have fun designing each month. You could create them in color schemes to suit the décor of a room or office; add photos to give a personal touch; follow a seasonal theme such as Christmas and Easter and include decorations for holidays; make them for sports teams; use photos of popstars, and actors; or make them to suit hobbies such as fishing, ballet, or football.

s	m	t	w	t	f	s
					1	2
3	4	5	6	7	8	9
10	11	12	13	14	15	16
17	18	19	20	21	22	23
24	25	26	27	28	29	30
31						

JUNE

11 When you have completed all twelve months (make sure February is on the reverse of January), use the sharp end of a pencil to punch through the paper to reveal the holes at the top of each one.

12 Thread the rings through the matching holes. Make sure you have laid out the months in order so that when you flip over each one you see the next consecutive month.

 **Ideas to try**

These can be cut and pasted, or the entire design including the calendar can be done on the computer.

Make your own designs on the computer, cut them out, and glue them on.

Use buttons, beads, and numbers for a fun look.

Simple ideas like strips of colored paper and stick-on letters are really neat.

Recycle old cards for cute photos and pictures.

Tips of the trade

It would be worthwhile to spend some time producing a few different samples of your work to show when selling. You could even create a catalog on the computer and use this to demonstrate how versatile the calendars can be.

Think about ways you can apply the same techniques involved in making desk calendars to grow your business.

Some examples of other ideas are wall calendars, height charts for children, reward charts for parents to use with their kids, and one-year-at-a-view desk mats. The possibilities are endless!

Heads up

"Keep a list of the people who buy a desk calendar from you and contact them again the following year to buy another one!"

 ## Talking cents

Be aware that it takes some time to make up each calendar. A good rule of thumb for setting your sale price is to combine the cost of materials with the time you spent to make the calendar. If it took you one hour, then you can set a rate such as $10 per hour.

$10 per hour for time + materials = $ Cost to charge

 ## Marketing your business

You could market your calendars to businesses as the end of the financial year (June 30) approaches, to families and individuals as the calendar year comes to an end.

Saving and spending

Once you start making some extra cash, it is important that you manage your money wisely. There's nothing worse than finding you have nothing to show for all that hard work.

It is never too early to learn about the value of money and how to budget and save. With more money to spend and more opportunities to spend it, you can easily get into financial trouble. So before those coins burn a hole in your pocket, listen to a few financial tips.

Saving your $$$

Set a goal for something special you would like to buy.

Plan ahead for unexpected expenses related to the business or something personal like a friend's birthday.

Save any loose change you have in a jar – it's surprising how quickly it mounts up. This money could be useful for buying gifts and for any other expenses you may not have planned for.

Put savings goals in writing to make them seem more real. You might even want to show these goals to a parent. Being held accountable for your goals can help you stay on track.

Try the 50/50 rule – save 50% of your money and spend 50%!

Cut back on expenses (e.g., rent a DVD to watch with friends rather than go to the movies).

Set goals that are based on your values, not on keeping up with what your friends have.

Open a savings account if you haven't already done so.

Budgeting

Budgeting involves understanding how much money you earn and spend over a period of time. When you create a budget, you are creating a plan for spending and saving money. Start by listing all your regular income (e.g., an allowance or earnings from a part-time job or business). Next, make a list of regular expenses. Subtract your expenses from your income. If the result shows that you won't have enough income to cover your expenses, you'll need to come up with a plan for making up the shortfall – or learn to live with spending less!

Spending your $$$

It takes so long to earn but is spent so quickly! You might want to invest some of your money back into your business by expanding, upgrading equipment, or advertising in local papers.

Buy wisely – look around for the best deals or wait for an item to go on sale.

Think through spending decisions rather than buying on impulse. If you like something, then leave the store and take time out, or even come back the next day. When you go back to the store in a different frame of mind, you'll know if you still want the item.

Learn to identify the difference between want and need. You might want something but do you really need it?

Always go to your parents or another suitable adult for information, support, and advice.

Look out for more
cool titles at
www.tracymarsh.com

Published by Tracy Marsh Publications
Copyright © 2009 by Tracy Marsh Publications Pty Ltd

For any questions or queries, contact the publisher,
Tracy Marsh Publications
Norwood S.A. AUSTRALIA
Tel: 61 8 8363 1248

www.tracymarsh.com

Produced by Phoenix Offset
Printed in China

ISBN: 978 1875899 46 3 (pbk.)

Publisher: Tracy Marsh

Graphic Designer: Kel Gibb

Production Manager: Mick Bagnato